IF ARIEL DANCED
ON THE MOON

George,
Remembering fondly our
readings in the poetry
"heydays." ✳

Peace,

CHARLES R. BACHMAN

TRAFFORD
PUBLISHING™

Note for Librarians: A cataloguing record for this book is available from Library and Archives Canada at www.collectionscanada.ca/amicus/index-e.html
ISBN 1-4120-9012-1

Printed in Victoria, BC, Canada. Printed on paper with minimum 30% recycled fibre. Trafford's print shop runs on "green energy" from solar, wind and other environmentally-friendly power sources.

TRAFFORD
PUBLISHING™
Offices in Canada, USA, Ireland and UK

Book sales for North America and international:
Trafford Publishing, 6E–2333 Government St.,
Victoria, BC V8T 4P4 CANADA
phone 250 383 6864 (toll-free 1 888 232 4444)
fax 250 383 6804; email to orders@trafford.com
Book sales in Europe:
Trafford Publishing (UK) Limited, 9 Park End Street, 2nd Floor
Oxford, UK OX1 1HH UNITED KINGDOM
phone +44 (0)1865 722 113 (local rate 0845 230 9601)
facsimile +44 (0)1865 722 868; info.uk@trafford.com
Order online at:
trafford.com/06-0768

10 9 8 7 6 5 4 3

For Nancy

CONTENTS

ALONG THE SKUNK RIVER

Ever persistent, determined as any kingfisher
there beside where the water rushed
most swiftly edible treasures to pluck
out of its onflowing never the same fingers

out of the hands of its darkness its roiled substance
to lift out as treasure closed in a chest
in an ancient vessel far under the crest
of whatever waves moving, whatever surges

flung into dusk darkness as night approached
he flung out his several lines his lures
wrinkled forehead in flickered firelight
cautioning me his lad with soft voice

no one to let know this night or tomorrow
especially Game Warden
spoken with squinted eyes the same
almost as last Sunday, man's frail sorrow

at our God help us flawed failed being,
this to the heart of this eight years lad
edged similar awe inside
yes I nodded of course no such thing

would pass my lips. He smiled at having known
I would say it yet somehow glad
to hear it almost as if afraid
he wouldn't. Revelling in trust I wandered down

along the dark uncertain line of shore
hands gratefully touching the smooth
welcome of dry river-seasoned
driftwood which I carefully lifted, bore

back to stack on our weakly crackling fire.
What did we muse on, speak of then
in that flicker of flame water night shadow
weight of unlawful doings enhancing the waiting,
side by side on the wool blanket
hoping for catfish or bass by morning?

IN THE PINES

Just into the pines
not far from shore
the voice quickly rises
rapidly descends
in moments across
the barely wrinkled
water

Forest dirge
pining away
the lone wolf chants
his song of himself

at times
with the right wind
right mix of air and water
he seems, though distant,
immense back there
where even my hawkeye glasses
cannot penetrate

are unable to ferret out
even the dim outline
of his feral greyness
though sun has a hand-breadth
before it touches the tops of the conifers
spreads molten
dips down beyond the mountain.

He calls again
or is it she
from another enclave
answering from dimness to dimness
out of obscurity?

They both in turn
likely able to see quite clearly
able to wonder
why this sheen-eyed
two-legged creature
stands so still,
frozen, staring
as if to spring.

The Hedges, Blue Mountain Lake
October 4, 2005

DEEP IN OKTEONDON'S SPIRIT

When the beautiful Eagle Woman
lured him down into the hollow tree
Okteondon The Rooted One was not blithely naive
when he gave way to her invitation
to lay his head on her lap and go to sleep,

because just before drifting off
he tied one of his long black hairs
to a solid part of the inner trunk,
so that when, as he slept, she swept him
into a large parfleche bag and joltingly swept
upward with it toward the sky,
he was held, pulled back, by the hair,
woke up and asked her what had happened.

And though he went to sleep again at her request,
in spite of what she had tried, he was not
really foolish because deep in his spirit he sensed
a growing Orenda power that did not desert him
though she untied the hair
stuffed him into the parfleche and this time
soared out of the tree far up above
the craggy cliff, opening the bag, dropping him
onto the hardness of rocky ledge,

as he looked around and saw the pile of bones
and near-dead bodies turning into corpses
as Otgont eagles swept down, tore out chunks
of flesh, one tearing off a piece of his arm

his laughter was Orenda sign as he spit upon the wound
it healing immediately. He was not naive when
again he drifted to slumber, something deep in his spirit
told him to, and to trust the vision of his Spirit Protector
to plant a cedar twig nearby and a great cedar would grow
up which he could climb.

Upon awakening, when following the command
the great cedar grew to the cliff's summit
he was not merely impulsive to start the hickory
breaking over the bones and corpses, telling them
to hurry or it would fall on them because
deep in his spirit something told him they would
resurrect, rise, and climb with him up the long cedar
to the crag's summit safety and home.

And when he refused to remain with them
though all seemed now secure,
he was not foolish when he informed them
he had to go back to find his wife the Eagle Woman,
because something deep in his spirit
some Orenda intuition was assuring him of the curve
of his coming destiny, motioning him to destroy
the remaining Otgont destructive beings,

And when he saw again his beautiful Eagle wife
sitting with her mother he was not naive
to go up to her, be introduced because he sensed
his wife this time was truthful, as she took him aside,
warning him of her mother Kahenchitahonk
notorious Eagle Woman Witch, Okteondon
had the seemingly foolish but really wise good sense

to believe his wife and to submit to her mother's demand
that she the mother be obeyed in all things,
and he that night to pound the head
of the tossing and turning Kahenchitahonk with
the corn-pounder, and to agree on successive nights
to kill the maleficent White Beaver and Black Eagle,

Okteondon was not naive to the danger these creatures posed,
but in his spirit knew he would lay them at the Witch's feet
and in refusing to give the mother any part
but rather to dismember the corpses, invite in
to a Gaqsahon Eat-All-Feast the Dagwenoenyents
who were Whirlwind Flying Heads, deep in his mind
he knew they would eat and savor every last morsel
noting how delicious the bodies of Kahenchitahonk's
brother and husband had tasted,

He was not naive then nor earlier when
as a child, though his grandfather Haienthwus The Planter
had placed him under the roots of the great tree
to keep him safe from the Eagle Women
who had killed all his extended family,
Okteondon found himself singing a song of power
uprooting, overturning the great tree,
from which he did not die because deep in his spirit
he sensed his grandfather was right
with his gift of his own smoke-blackened
bow and the cedar flute with which he called
ever larger prey, bringing them down and
back to the lodge to nurture them both, and
when in spite of the old man's warning
not to go north he directed his steps there

anyway he was not stupid or foolish because
deep in his spirit he sensed a nurturant force
which drove him on to the hollow tree.

So when he obeyed even the final command
of the old woman he was not supremely naive
to step into the sweat lodge, be blocked in
as she sang her ancient song to make it red hot
because in his mind his spirit he sensed his Orenda
that would drive him out alive drive her in
to her fiery death only a harmless screetch owl escaping,
deep in his mind he sensed in all that his destiny
was curving around to complete the circle broken
by Otgont evil, reuniting those who had been lost,
and that this circle would also become
a force which far, far into the future
could repair the broken hoop of all his people.

MOUNTAINS

Thinning brows
on the face of this year
begin once more
their seasonal meddling
with each other

leaning inward
to press, ponder
between them a spare,
scowling geography.

Belatedly this year hears,
remembers what it was told
by the year before,

that the earth has grown older,
now less nearly resembles
a concentration
of etched Himalayas
firm above plain, plateau,

that no eruption
can balance
rain or hail
wearing down
brow, face
of rugged peaks,
deepening
ravines, arroyos.

Always too late
the year remembers.

Only after each cycle of seasons
does it open itself
to detect the echo,
speak its wrinkled truth
to its young
stone-eared
successor.

LETCHWORTH GORGE, EARTH MOTHER

From any one vantage point
the long opening
across her face
extends
as if forever.

Her river-carved, weathered carapace
frowns, smiles
depending on the place
we look from.

No matter where upon her
we place our feet
the depths out of which she speaks
clothed in vastness remain
warm, granitic, sibylline.

CAPE COD DUNE BEACHES

Long twist of water
tears velocitous
along dusky shore
from dim eastern promontory

accelerating
engine ever slashing
with ever more thunder
terror, intermittent flash

snake dervish whirling
long aqua monster
gobbling the sandy verge
slicing up to rapt audience

who feel an ecstatic urge
to embrace its magnificence
be voracious for
its incessant purgings:

expanding in-tides
fascinatingly
unforeseeable
pools roiling inward

from ocean marge
soaking us up to
unforeseeable body bumps and inlets
threatening to rush is into the surge

as we flash out small monster
screams fearful, festive,
dying out as the wild corkscrew clamor
recedes down the western shore
to a dirg-ish tremor.

RACE POINT BEACH

Ripple-clutter piles
detritus-ornamented
mini-hills valleys arroyos
lace sand with treasured

miscellany:
dead, half-alive
greenish fetid mollusks,
seaweed whose scent

sun-dries in minutes
leaving in salt-fresh air
faint whiff of cigarette butts
civilizations's moist
fragrant gift.

FURY

Ridgely wizened
face of Rock
on side of cliff
in hazy dusk light
smiles out over
his ancient neighbor Sea
as He has done for eons,
anticipating
their in-tide
wave sound echo
conversation
as his old friend
assumes his usual
liveliness at evening.

Far below
well-distanced outward
Wind lashes languid Water
into hackles of ploughed sillion
that rise, gather
push, increase

rank upon rank
phalanxes building endlessly
out of the deep
as if into battle
front ranks being destroyed
torn apart as they hit the shore

more and more continue to rise
in their marching dance
higher, faster,
with ever-greater momentum
grimly ever-less-fearful army
surging far past the beachhead
each rank more gigantic

frenzy of mad erosion
tearing away sand, pebbles,
assaulting cliff itself
drowning out the startled voice
of Rock attempting to reply
as He becomes fragments
raining down
washing out
with eve-tide water
into the Maelstrom.

GLORIES OF MORNING

The green-leaved presence climbing a taut string
is with its siblings a glory of morning
a beauty of dawn midday and dusk.

When it climbs a stalk of sweet corn in the ploughed field
pulling tightly, encompassing stalk, leaf, and budding ear
it is a sneaky, suffocating, noxious thing.

When sprigs of maize life-staff sprout
their aggressive light green in a myrtle bed
they must be yanked out as strange intruders.

Pointy-leaved deep-green classic-laden myrtle
may make its unwelcome presence known
little by little in the soft sweet woodruff
surrounding a blooming rose of sharon.

With surprising speed tops of the biblical sharon
rise up unwelcome sprigs of unshaven whisker
beneath delicate morning glories in full flower.

PEONY

as green freshness of bud cover loosens
finger by finger peeling away
splaying outward ends drooping down
and moist mass of pink barely fragrant

begins to differentiate segment itself
what a leavening is fermenting
filling stem receptacle ovule
transforming delicate infant parchment

shapes into layers of curved wonder
as petals fanlike unfold lay themselves
open to night coolness dawn dew
midday sun and rain and wind

to eye smiles that catch their light
to shy breath inspirations that take in
layer on layer of densely rich scent
drifting downward through throat and body
into the full depths of my soul in spring.

WINDED INSTRUMENTS

Let autumn winds
play maples and pines
as if they were cellos
let the cellists dig in
producing warmer sounds
let bows resonate leaved strings
ever more strongly until
towering instruments bow
beneath these unrelenting
haired dervishes
and all strings are severed
for one more turn of nature.

INSERTION

Two weeks ago when we left
for a trip out East the little
silver maple seemed to be
thriving behind the arbor,

its light green, smooth-edged,
elongated leaves promising
a steady, vigorous growth
with uniform bark, foliage

to simply grow taller, larger
as Mother Earth and Father Sky
showed their seasonal kindness.
Imagine our dismay when

upon returning, a limb
unlike the others had risen
out of the small trunk, grafted
but blended so skillfully

with the mother stem we couldn't
tell where one began, the other
ended. Its bark is rougher,
coarser, scratchy to the touch,

its leaves elongated much
more sharply, pointed, with subtle
but unmistakable saw-toothed
edges, but more palely yellowed.

Its angle from the
still-tentative trunk is so
acute that it points almost straight
skyward as if with growing

it will by its very shape
and apparent vigor become
the mother trunk. But supposing
it somehow inserts its sharp-toothed,

rough-barked progeny throughout
our loved, prized sprig of beauty,
transforming it into something
we no longer recognize?

WHEN FINE GREEN DOWN

When fine green down
on breast of meadow
turns to brownish stubble

does heart within
begin slower tempo
knowing she is
unleavening herself
for coming slumber?

When downy feathers
on head and neck
of sugar maples
turn sun and fire

is head planning
that throat's song
will be matching counterpoint
to soaring colors
of demise?

WHEN REPTILES AND SUCH, SPEAK

When reptiles and such, speak
in tongues as it were
or when they observe us
in whatever way
it may behoove us to be cautious, to listen, to be attentive.

Crocodile clacks its buon giorno cuspidly
with intake of air, eyes us
for response.
Alligator almost
the same, maybe a bit more air?
The difference is subtle but he is staring too.

Now the monitor seems
     to let his tongue
        loll
           and
             swiggle
        (a
       salivary
     hiss?)
as his dinosour structure sways
ever so slightly   back and forth.
He is keeping   tabs on us.

Salamanders
and newts on the other
hand when they know they've
been spotted suddenly lose their
camouflaged poise,
darting for the nethermost
regions they can manage,
uttering soft, angry
remonstrances.
From hidden
shelters
though
they
may
be
watch
-ing.

Similarly,
garters, milk snakes,
the small fry
of their group
pay close
attention
to sight,
vibration,
snaking
away
if
they
can

while flicking lightning electric
tongues
that whisssssssssssssssssssssssssper, "asshole!"
And from
under the grass, debris,
their bodies are listening, listening.

ON THE OTHER HAND ANACONDAS
PYTHONS, THE MUCH LARGER SORT
ARE NOT AT ALL QUICK TO HURRY AWAY.
NO SIR, THEIR SHEER GIGANTIC MIGHT
ALLOWS THEM THE LEISURE TO BE STILL,
ATTENTIVE, WAITING FOR US WHO MAY NOT HEAR
THEIR MUTED MULTI-BELLY ACID RUMBLE.

Rock, tree lizards,
especially rock ones
are still, like stones, crags,
  branches they may seem wedded to.
    But don't be fooled by this masquerading.
    They are ever vigilant as they
  murmur   under   their   breath
   eons   of   wis   dom
  about us   recent   inter   lopers.

Turtles
of all kinds
share in such stasis
but to lesser degree since
they must maneuver in land
and water   and they remember,
especially the large North American
one, who will always   speak and act
kindness as long as we   listen to its
ancient advice as it remembers
how it supported us all as we
came to life in the verdent
earth on its great mosaic
shell.

CRICKET SONG

The small zone
within which
voiced crickets
were forbidden
seemed to some
to expand

as the inner circle
rippled outward
like a living
perimeter-army
threatening safety
unfree-

ing all crickets
who thought their chirping
fresh, eternal
ever of spring
guaranteed
lit

with spirit fire.
They hop, scramble
into, over
each other in headlong
panicked flight
each

ever more intent
on saving the self,
some more aware
pretend to lose
their proud voices,
mime

a silence, in case
in case in case.
Others try
to fight the grim
invisible enemy
losing

ground and energy
with each blow.
Chirping voices
volume down,
symphonic flow
ceases

nearly as mimes
hop into the ripple
they jumped away from
holing up in the
voiceless womb
belonging

till one lone
chirper stands
outside the perimeter
of holy silence
singing singing
softer

SPRING

The yellow butterfly flutters
on a small branch, unaware
among lush leaves
that she lacks camouflage.
Her wings whisper in the still air
as behind her eyes
the bird descends, brushing her plumage

gently a moment before
he claws the soft tube of her body.
She does not sense
the grey approach, her twin
antennae, dulled in the balmy haze, miss
the whirr of wing. Torn

now in the monstrous noise
of relentless beak and claw
the butterfly enlarges, turns,
her wings now wider than falcons,
suddenly gluing her legs to the maw
of the startled bird.
Her poised limbs
do their work in silence

deaf to chirping, pressing,
pressing gently on
down to a flutter
as the dark proboscis
fragrant still with nectar
quiets the faint trembling
of beak and tongue.

CRAB

When soft prey slithers
within my clawish purview

I wait, still.
As if sensationless.
Closer
it swirling swims.
Now.

Split-secondly
I open
extend
my talons.
Snap.

Neither my serrated claws
nor pronged eyes
sense whiff or notion
of flesh jelly nurturance.

Pang:
crustacean vexation.
Zing:
dentalian deprivation.

Me:
hubrissy locomotion
stirring up clouds
of sea-bottom dust
honing in on nothing
snapping with random
maniacal mastication

gone awry
my ancient cretacious core
as I fail to feel
the faint ocean tremor
of my own looming masticator.

FEATHERED FORMS

Thrush's wings are able sometimes
to air-swimming sing and sing
away even hardest coldest winter winds
with those pitched echoes finding

their way to gentle the earth-walkers
into an early spring,
resonating their almost unheard tones
within the beings within

even before throated songs
have let their more obvious pitches ring
into us two-legged four-legged many-legged
crawling slithering swimming

creatures who have as always
awaited with muted yearning
what these repeating yet new-sprung wonders
would be permitted to bring.

NESTING

Her pained wings
carry her slowly
toward his nest,
the torn plumage
of her last union
forms a long trail behind her
descending wisp by wisp to the ground.

The warmth of his own
freshly-healed wings
around her seems
to lessen the hurt,
then
in time
wounds open again.

She moves out
from beneath,
perches for moments tensely
on his nest's perimeter

glides haltingly
to a ledge nearby,
her injured rudder
balancing her precariously
on the narrow edge,

Her keen eyes sense the long drop to the hard clay below.

Her limp wing tells her
if she loses balance
plummets downward
she will not have
the strength to soar
upward again.

Open rescue wings
eagerly beckon
from other nests--
short distance,
near enough
to glide to
with little effort
if she lifts off
correctly
and does not fall.

There as she hoped with him
it might be warm, safe,
here on the precipice
cold, dangerous,

Her wounds hurt less,
seem to be healing.

VIBRATIONS

Faint emanations
seem to issue
from a band
of laminated
grass-green
cicadas

a choral ring
almost nothing
oozes forth
from underneath
the clam-tight
plastic shell

or is it fancy,
that apparent sigh,
or listened to
more intently
almost a cry
as of distant fright

or wished-for flight
back into trees
of paradise
before the capture,
the locking-in,
the squeezing out

of night air laden
with nurturant mystery
of odors, shadow,
cacophanic symphony.

Something squeezes forth
still, still,
a thread, threads
microscopic waves
of thrum, tingle
assert their voices

until the people
itch with undefined
irritation, scratching
near-deaf ears
reddening faces,
squeezing, sealing more firmly
the plastic coffin.

CLINGER

Small ruffled mass of black
seemingly stuck to the inside
wall of our refreshing
swimming pool under

the metal projecting rim
just over the square
water intake opening
utterly still in the morning

large leaf adhered by moisture
I thought, so I found a dead
hollow wild phlox stem,
walked around the outside

to just the right of where
the leaf would be clinging
(could not see it at that angle
because of the rim's lip overhang)

poked it to loosen so it would
plummet into the keen
encompassing water, to then
be skimmed up and flung

into the yard. My tentative poke
seemed greeted by a small sound—
my ears crackling?
congested water suction?

A second gentle jab elicted
the mutter a bat makes when cornered,
threatened, or in pain.
I ventured back to where I could see,

noted small elfin ears,
nose moving down toward water,
up again into stillness. A fluke?
By daylight caught unawares,

therefore roosting until nightfall?
I would wait and see, hoping
the following morning
would find it gone.

No such good fortune then,
so for our easing and mercy
unpleasant necessity raised its head
calling to me in its always grim voice.

Making cautious preparation
I flung it with skimmer onto
nearby grass. Still as ice.

Gentle poke with skimmer,
only head and mouth
could move, making a throatier
squeak than the day before.

No choice but with a blow
of metal yard rake
to plunge its tormented self
suddenly into its own afterlife

as I whispered a prayer
for its safe journey.
Then with a single motion
bagged and in the container.

There in a strange safety
even if its tantalizing aroma
could be detected, outdoor fellow
creatures, our favorite Tom,

other felines, assorted woodchucks,
crows oppossums, racoons,
would not likely feast on
its possibly rabid remains.

———————————————————

Until I found out they could be released
by closing doors, leaving windows open
I cornered, killed them with dustpan and broom
in churches, basements, homes I have known.

Sonarly sensitive, silent, speedy
masters of maneuvering,
why do they enter where they disturb
fright-prone two-legged humans?

these near us
kill thousands of pesky mosquitoes
bother no one
mainly keep to themselves,

creatures who never once
get snarled into one's hair
or engage in other than
group feeding, socializing,

an impressive tribe of responsible,
interactive, well-meaning beings
who must often wonder

who these large-headed large-eyed
others are making strange sounds
beneath one's evening home.

So now this small one lies
inert, enclosed, while I hope
for the sake of all its outdoor
fellow beings including its
clan brothers and sisters

its disease if it had one was only
unto itself, that now its soul
can consume spirit mosquitoes,
roost and soar as it wills.

RABBIT TO CHIPMUNK

Fast heart-beatened
almost past enduring
chased harrassed
by enemies more scary
for seeming at times
to lack identity
and are therefore
evil potently

thank Rabbit-God
who led me to the hollow
in this bulky spruce
dim rotting warm safe
the opening far too small
for them.

Opposite me
barely seen
in this dark enclosure
someone sits
makes quiet sound

I wait
glance his way
will he notice me
he goes about his business
munching on something succulent
I stare and speak
he is into himself his food

I speak again
louder
make gesture

no response

He does not follow
the decency code
if he did
he would emit
reassuring sounds
though our languages are
different surely he would
make a sign
broad enough
to show I am welcome.

He moves his head
notices me
that is all.
Even meanest creatures
follow the decent code
guestship hospitality
like-mindedness
patriotism of small places

especially since we two alone
share this besieged nestle
especially since he is smaller
more vulnerable
to outside enemies
for whom he should feel

the same
blood-pumping hatred
as I

His refusal
to behave with even
basic Rabbitry
Animality
shows he must be waiting
to betray me to those
dangerous strangers
damn him my heartbeat
is again at panic level

I have no choice but to act
with rightful resolution
evict this immoral interloper
who carries the stench of corruption,
he is beyond the pale
as seen when he seems unmoved
even as I justly thrust him
out of my dark rotting
warm secure
homeland.

RABBIT IN THE STARS

There suddenly between
Orion and something else
Constellation Lepus again
through atmospheric haze
ovular face
with harelip shape
as myriad star pattern coalesces

chest paws imagined rest of body
one that strangely—
lop-ears cocking? eyes darting
nose twitching,

eyes focus on us
as ours on it
not possible

what sort of
rabbit of stars is this?
massive head turning
back and forth
and now again to us
momently
we turn our eyes away

as through thin cloud
the shape the full
configuration emerges
stellar hare
standing fur like
bristling boar hair

lop-eared mobile albino wraith
in black desert
full of glistening
grains of sand,

swamp ghost racing
through stellar bayou mist
glitter eyes
mouth tooth-jagged
the essence of itself
hare! hare!

No closing of eyes,
act of reverse imagination
can halt your smoky trajectory
hurtling now at us
all the gestalt
we imagined
out of otherwise
scattered stars,

No Chippewa trickster
Nanabozho are you,
with incandescent tail
stealing fire
from the Great One,
nonetheless you seem
to be bringing
fire smoke what else
into us that thought of you

now too late too late
rabbit down from stars
teeth ears
eyes paws
upon us.

COYOTE'S LUCKY CHANCE

It sounded like it could be
somethin damned fortunate
somethin to lift my state
to make me feel like me

again, I felt it when I first
spied Cousin Fox up there
on top of that hill where
he was lookin like he'd burst

with some kind a great wonder
he was starin at way down below,
till his eyes looked like they'd blow
clean out of their sockets, thunder

right down hard over that hill,
till even suspicious me had to ask
hey Cousin up there, what task
you plannin, you look so still

and besides, grinnin from ear to ear?
When he yelled his kind answer
I thought then and there for sure
my ship had come in, no more fear

of hunger, of any of my hungers,
no sir, so I looked where he said
ran down to that there lake bed
this time knowin down to my fingers

It was gonna show itself, gonna come in
as soon it did, that great big delicious-
lookin piece of fry bread, more lucious
surely than anything this starvin, thin

animule called Coyote had ever seen.
And it got bigger, and as per his
yelled instructions, I slurped and sucked this
lake water, and dude I really mean

sucked it up and in, makin that feast
edge closer and closer, my pitiful belly
growlin because it had felt empty
since I had had to scarf the least

fleshy of mangy prairie dogs that other
time, well anyway to make a long story
brief, as soon as that wonderful, glori-
ous frybread come close, the water

splashed and rippled and it was gone.
Yup. Fox laughin his asshole head off
cause he threw the rock that poof!
made it disappear under the risin moon.

TWISTED CHIMERA

To arrive at the twisted remains
of a well-ribbed chimera
involves a highly-processed trajectory
beginning with the sighting
distantly clued by its shadow song

overcoming natural qualms
that emerge unwelcome
assessing the apt distance
to initiate echo
eye-scouring the forbidding silhouette

all senses alert for an answer
then when it shimmers
across the distance as its vague figure
seems to bestir
itself in the muted tumult of reply,

poising oneself to edge closer
because its reponse
seems to permit a movement nearer
I lessen the space
between myself and the dim creature

pretending a positive glow
to its invitation
concealing my weapon and true intention,
growing bolder
as its now near presence seems a smile,

(o what a shouting of praise
will be mine
to display the remains of this mythical creature
once is accomplished
the crushing victory I will attain)

must be extra clandestine
discipline down
the dangerous surge
within

I stealthily start
to unsheathe
the blade anointed with foul anti-chimera
medicine
when suddenly looms the shadow expanding
all in an instant engulfing blade and me
still with calmness still with smiling.

MAN SPIDER, SPIDER MAN

Where does it begin?
Achilles fascination
existence brave
brief, free
And he was on
revenge rescue
mission certainly,

Helen the victim
Paris vile abductor
perhaps only seducer
does it matter?
He was powerful
testosterone male
the hated other.
In either case
he done her wrong
and he must face
the music by playing
villain in Homer's
long song.

Like Captain Marvel
wondrous Batman
brave Achilles
I cannot stand
injustice,

like an even greater One,
more glorious than Achilles
greater because this me this one
whose passion is real
will now subsume
into modern epic--
without the Homeric hero's heel.

My position
in gene-research lab
gained me trust
for clandestine
needle fluid intake
into my veins,
a taste of puissance.

My very first Helen:
un-Helen-like blonde,
delicately winsome
when she informed me
what had occurred,
who was hounding her
in spite of her pleas.

I had second thoughts
only once
beholding his
brazen expression,
muscled tatoos
as he swaggered
toward her place
to abuse her again

or worse.

He struck me once.
That was all
he had time for.

The surge I experienced
at whom I had saved
as I perceived
that in seconds
it would be over
neither I nor Homer
would be able
to say in a poem.

My dose of serum
had been
so infinitesimal
as in my expert opinion
to virtually guarantee
my power would remain
within Batman-Achilles realm,
not lead to
arachnid unforeseen.

As other triumphs followed
the words in my head
seemed to realign.
Effort was more minimal
potency more free
as I came to expect
tender gratefulness

leading, I hoped,
to the perfect she for me.

Thought was transpiring
less and less,
but more and more
there seemed to be
in maidens' eyes
fear confounding
my wilderness,

driving me to aspire beyond
my chivalrous calling,
my high ideal.
Could this greater need possess
the germ of loving ravenousness?

But yes, I history re-perused--
One cannot an omelette make
unless some eggs one break,
still alive was the golden quest,
still throbbing the maiden breast
that me would thank with bliss
For bringing rescue, happiness!

So on, though broken eggs
increased with power of web
that from my own chest emanated,
like flies I them ensnared
and I my great fangs bared
as with their fluids mine were sated.

But within me twisting
a remnant of my nature pushing
my surging mind-self, saying
un-nature was compelling
me on through means
that had become
ideals themselves
the only quest
a shell of power
an emptiness.

And so I ferreted out
to hunt and terrorize
a pyromaniac
with no fear in his eyes,
then standing still
I essayed his game,
let him engulf
this Achilles in flame.

PATCHES

We have a calico cat whose fur
is comprised entirely of batches
of reddish black rust and white
and thus we call her Patches.

Sometimes when she is fiery
I like to call her Matches
as she skirmishes with Lily
her enemy/friend, whose matches

with her are ended by closure
of her whom I now dub Latches
because she has basically locked it up
and thus avoided (serious) scratches

for either. But sometimes as she sleeps
I decide to call her Hatches
because some plot seems afoot,
then I think of her also as Catches

because it may involve bird or mouse
and then her dream attaches
itself to her body which flickers
and then she is Watcho-McBatcho

because all bets are off and she
has by now completely detachoed
the faintest traces of finest feline feminine sanity
from her now grossly mismatchoed

mind so she is a true
feline Wacko-Watcho
whose seeming inner tranquility
at the moment seems all dispatcho

(Besides, she looks exactly like a
Wacko-Watcho-McBatcho)

and sometimes during these spells
her fur rises to a kind of thatch
making her a large and very
scary abominable Saskwatch,

and then par bleu! She makes
a sudden, miraculous snatch
of her serenity, and once more
becomes—my familiar Patch.

SNIFFING BY WOODS
(With apologies to Robert Frost)

Whose woods these are I think I know,
He must be in the pasture though,
Too bad for him, I'm stopping here
To catch his scent upon the snow.

His markings are too faint, I fear,
They make my sniffer veer and veer
Between the woods and frozen lake
The coldest evening of the year.

I give myself a warming shake,
Thinking this search a big mistake,
When to my nose comes suddenly
A pungent scent that makes me quake.

The woods are silent, dark to me,
But I have urges to make me free,
And many marks on which to pee,
And many marks on which to pee.

INFERNO

There is a wondrous creature that seems wired as
nothing we can remember seeing before,
Its apparent mission to keep us mired as

deeply as possible in worry and the direst
doldrums of health decrepitude and more,
with more variations than a Bach concerto, this virus

utilizes every single one to bore
its sharp, merciless proboscis into our heads,
our drying throats, our hacking chests, our sore

and steaming bronchia weighted like lead
when we sit, lie down. And when after days
of slowness to table to bathroom, back to bed,

we feel a tinge of wellness, a break in the haze
of torporous phlegmy brain, of snotty rheum,
and rise up one fine morning, quite amazed

to be finally rid of the nuisance and all its gloom,
shower, dress, and with only a small cough
be off to rejoin the living, feeling the bloom

of the day once again, ready and willing to quaff
life's vintage, that's when the sonovabitch will show
its true Machiavellian smarts, its venal trough

of poisonous swill it has held in its sneaky burrow
inside our bones, our muscles, arteries, veins,
a swill no hog or man should ever know

as it spurts upward, turdish fountain of wolfsbane
re-invading with evil, cackling glee
(I can hear its fanatical yuk yuk at each new pain),

all of our upper regions--our fervent plea
and *Scheisskopf maledetto* asshole fuck you curse
notwithstanding, it brings us back to our knees
and this time what the hell bring on the hearse.

COMPANY REVEILLE

Much to be desired is:
a magic reveille in which one's
ideas feelings histrionics
will as one man
at my commanded call
gather promptly for muster
all their ranks and kinds
neatly spaced alloted filed
in front of a gleaming barracks wall,
each starched figure, face
eager to task itself
according to its apt placing,
anxious to please
that which, each trusts,
lies in that within my soul
which is guaranteed to make of them
by God! an effective army of the aesthetic will!

Such reveille is reverie,
since gathered here are a dank-eyed, blear-brained lot
in lines resembling the chalked zig-zags
of a hung-over teacher's blackboard geometry
in varying stages of deshabille,
no knowledge of
feeling for
any tasks
whatsoever
and, in a motley
of un-uniform uniforms

from assorted
companies
battalions
divisions
armies
nations.

My inner Company Commander
reaches inside his clamped helmet
to tear the wisps of hair that remain,
asking himself if ever there has been
such a lot as his lot,
such motley as his motley,
whom in the course of one day's
bodywash brainwash drill and supply
he tries to devise, revise
into something Mars could tolerate,
only to see with next morning's bugle refrain
the same menage again.

ENGRAVING

It etched its way
into my memory
like the feet of a large
unwelcome toad
on the moist ground
of a prissy person's
spring garden.

FRIEND IN ALL WEATHERS
(1974)

The shadow of loneliness
has a peculiar habit
of darting like a large, swift spider
out of its unseen enclosure
when it is least expected

springing up huge, ghost-like, near the light
covering my narrow room
with the sudden immensity
of its darkness

its body holding my floor's center
an amorphous stain
its legs extending to all corners
to everything between the corners.

Holding, holding,
my walls absorb its blunt silence
awaiting its slow shrinkage
away from the light

to its exclusive domain
without apparent injury
ready to return
when it whims.

IYA

That thing
that lies in the tall grass
just beyond the edge
of my well-mown
field.

That thing
that seems to swim, rippling
the dark, watery border
of my clear wading
stream.

That thing
that leaves its uneven tracks
on the extreme shoulder
of my familiar
path.

That thing, that waif
that claws scurrying
from outbush to outbush
tearing through dreams
crying to be fed.

PARTICLES

When a man living alone
returns to his reluctant house
the frown of his living room
nudges its way into him.

Unlike the sturdy self
he left outside standing,
his present vessel shatters
against walls that enclose him.

He cannot mend it. Quickly
he moves to retrieve the other.
Between his feet and the door
shards of himself have heaped into scowls

he cannot climb. Outside the light
has ended, night rescinds
the one, embraces the frown,
leaving him suspended.

DEATH ROW
(DECEMBER 12, 1974)

Bullets of hard light
shaft through my hesitant window
each time the night
without and within
refuses to remain
warm and motionless.

Each time they appear well-aimed
at carefully-selected
sites of memory
releasing from walls of sleep
the most colorful,

bizarre prisoners
some of whom
I would have sworn
were serving a life sentence.
Their motley selves protest
their innocence
as they emerge
grimacing.

To no avail.
Again it is time,
the brilliant dawn of execution
seems to have come

with no apparent fanfare, throng
to blunt the irrevocable light
with pageantry,
as, masked in twisted smiles,
they fall in muster
outside the massive doors

of their confined safety.
Suddenly, because of an apparent
act of regal mercy,
they begin returning
as always,
their new-laughed faces

now drawn, cornered,
to their familiar cells
and frowning warden
who had thought them justly
finally punished and laid to rest.

FRAGMENTIA PRAECOX: TO THE POWERS THAT BE
(LYRICS FOR POSSIBLE MUSIC 1974)

In the beginning was the word. St. John the Divine

The word, baby, it's the end. Unknown Author

Nowhere to go
no one to see
nothing to do.
Tell me if you
happen to know
what happened to me.

Or if you see part of me
floating by on air
or lolling down from a limb,
Give me a call
so I can rush there
and join this part with him.

Or if you see part of me
a giftless, unwise man
wandering after no star,
haunting the university
like the ghost of Dylan Thomas
haunting a bar,

Whisper a prayer
to the Mother of Darkness
so she'll tell me
where I are.

Just leave a little of me
to go haunting the silly streets,
to avoid, when it needs to,
its womb-tomb-room,
to eyeball a stranger it meets.

But if you see bits of me
cluttering space
with useless music
trying to shore up
a lonely time,
Give a tip to Divine Diana
to tear me away from my warm pi-ana
and the comfort of my rhyme.

Whisper a prayer
to the Mother of Darkness
so she'll tell me
where I are.

Whisper a plea
if you give a damn
so she'll let me
know who I am

LET YOURSELF

Let yourself grow old
let raindrops fall
let rate of droppage increase
let drops become threads
creeks streams rivers

as summers lengthen
let their dry beds deepen
as like a clever farmer
you till and plant
against eros-

ion that carves your smooth face
into line-fractures
ravines valleys
but patching frantically
you listen for

tremors volcanoes
signs of prolonged heat
in the inner core to throw up
lava soil
to replenish
your harried surface

and like ponce de
leon you find no
volcano or
gully glue or ra-

vine cement or hope-
long cassidy to
relieve you but
listen to

maya telling you
if you were cracking
it would be shameful
but fortunately
it is all maya

SEEKER

He thought he would search for perfection through variety.
Satiety might then emerge
like an extra appendage out of the womb.
If he worked at it long enough,
this variety,
the other might come.

The move of his mind and body
assumed the deliberate swing of a crane
lifting, placing
concrete stone on stone.

He continued.
After one structure another
and another.

They began to resemble each other
except in the size of their rooms.

He hurried on,
trying with speed to enrich
the blend of his being.
Confusion in the mix.
First one foot, then the other—
concrete blocks.

He slowed his pace.

His feet anchored to earth.

Still he could swing at the steel joint of his pelvis.
His mind could turn.
He planned and built
what was possible.

When his pelvis froze into poured concrete
he used his arms and neck to continue.

When these too went the way of the others
he took note but did not panic.
There were still his mouth his nose
his eyes his ears his brain.

A cloud of cement dust blew into his mouth, hardening.
Sand drifted into his nostrils and ears.
His eyes in their sockets glazed to glass.
His brain in its cage turned to stone.

He was bewildered, no doubt, by the change.
But perhaps he would not be displeased.
His form is unique and remains.
His poetry.

SUPERSEDED

If I am to be replaced eliminated
for another, if I as valued human
being of wisdom am to be
supplanted, how much better
to at least have been exchanged,
substituted, swapped, traded,

words which bear tones of evenness,
continued usefulness by items bartered.
But so it never really is, such interchange,
such evenness being mythic purely.

So my present state--all the worse because
it means one is somehow out of date,
out of what is momently thought significant,
ah but what does any moment of time know
of wisdom? thus superseded may indeed

be a complimentary virtue, depending on
the protean depths of those doing the superseding,
and if indeed they prove as surface-bound
as most such superseders, then I as superseded
have by reverse value become super-seeded,
better than tenth or even second seed
in the life tournament where to win
seems in our Zeitgeist to be everything--

Ah! to be superseded-super-seeded
in such a time means passing ones seeds
that some term seediness
into and on and after to that time when
what is now the un-supersedable will become
replaced eliminated supplanted obsolete
and I will be ceding nothing of the credit
I am to my race and species,
to the very idea of unsupersedableness.

THE PROFOUNDEST POEM EVER WRITTEN

Mots, etes-vous des mythes, et pareils aux myrthes des morts?
                                                    --Roger Desnos

He motions
emotions
by potions
of ocean
devotion.

His notion
of lotion
is cōscion
and grōssion.

To the slack
of attack
who having no back
avoid the rack
his lack
of a lack
has an arrogant smack.

He has a knack
of showing the hacks
the packs
they wear on their backs
and for this the slack
have called him a quack
yak yak.

THE WHITE STUFF

I dont give a crap what you say bud
the snow is comin the white
cold stuff I can smell
the flakeness to the back of
my nose bud and that tingle

is never wrong no matter
what you say bud and yours trulys
skin the old facial epidermis can
feel that windness even when
theres no wind that windness that

brings it on and down bud so
dont tell me its just gonna be
cold rain or some such shit cause
you know like I told you my old
mug and derriere theyre reliable bud

and I hate the thought goddamn another
year bringing this shit its too much
bud I already feel the naked singe
on my whole self so what the fuck
Im gonna get naked as a jay bird bud

and let the old bod venture out
and just recline on terra firma as
pop sky dumps his crapola load
on me all them flakes all that cold stuff
bud just bring it on just bring it on

THERE WAS THIS GUY

There was this guy with a crazy
look on his face kind of like
a would-be pancake in the last
stages of batter roil before
being slapped on the griddle yeah

even before the bubbly soon-to-be
doneness starts, for sure a long
ways before the telltale holes that
signal time to turn which always
makes you look forward to exactly what

kind of wavy tree-trunk rings etc.
this flip will show 'cause the speedup aging
is always wow no this guy's face was well before
that stage of cooking damn it made you
think its batter-y wobbles could go

any which way better watch it bud
every second 'cause if it shakes a certain
way with even more gooey pent-up-ness
it just might splatter out at you get on your
skin, crapola, soak you in man suffocate you

VILLANELLE FROM THE CITY

He never stopped to sense what was passing him by.
So caught up had he been in the daily grind
that once, when delayed by traffic he glanced at the sky;

it was a surprise: he'd always thought he was sly,
street-wise, alert to everything, not so blind
that he wouldn't fail to sense what was passing him by

if there was anything there to verify
the high opinion he had of his ranging mind:
so lucid he had no need to glance at the sky,

but there they were--some ragged cumuli
pushed so rapidly by the cold west wind,
he was forced to wonder if something had passed him by

because the deepening azure seemed so to vie
with the power of the clouds, he was unable to find
a way to absorb that thing that his glance at the sky

was revealing, it left him feeling cold and dry
for the first time ever, somehow left behind
in floundering anger at what may have passed him by,
at the cursed intrusion caused by that glance at the sky.

VILLANELLE FROM THE COUNTRY: BEING CAUGHT

Hide and seek we three decided to play,
I, my cousin Donna, her sister Carol Ann,
We'd take whatever risks that came our way

to select the darkest, most fascinating array
of hard-to-discover alcoves and chambers when
hide and seek we three commenced to play.

Donna was on her own against us--she'd convey,
as the oldest, the greatest mystery, making keen
the thrill of all the risks that came our way.

We finally uncovered her under a pile of hay
infested with mites and mice, and one large opossum
that almost halted the game we'd decided to play,

but escaping without any bites, though in disarray,
as Donna counted, Carol and I ran
toward the red hog-feeders, knowing the risks that came
   our way

getting stuck in the tiny space. It was not horseplay
when I sat on a wasp's nest, fled toward home getting stung
with regret that hide and seek we'd decided to play
for the oh-so-thrilling risks that came our way.

BUILDING FOUNDATION

Working construction daily in the hot sun,
sweating while loading, wheeling, pouring concrete,
hurrying eight to noon, lunch break till one,

sending the coagulant mass down twenty feet
into squarish ditches made by steel forms
trip after tiring trip until the neat

foundation began to take shape within its warm,
hard enclosure, itself matching the hardening
until a Gibralter-like firmness became the norm

of its substance, with layers continually pouring
over, into it, raising its level closer
to the ultimate goal, the foundation's summit, the ring

of sweaty victory we all were ordered to strive for
as we rushed the heavy wheelbarrows toward
our destination, pushing them rapidly under

the giant rolling drum of wet sand
and white cement, until they were almost full,
prone to tip over and spill at the slightest

move off-balance, us keeping the roil
steady as we almost ran along the narrow
board platform toward our pouring fall

place, hands, arms, shoulders, elbows
straining to pull then push the barrow's handles
upward so the living substance would flow

smoothly down between its faithful walls.
Aching, we longed for rest and took our wages
often forgetting, amidst our sweaty haul
we were pouring a church's solid rock of ages.

HOEING SOYBEANS I

down and up another sweaty row
from the end not a blessed bean in sight
endless line of cockleburrs that were so

jungle intermeshed thick and tight
it was hard to bend and swing the corn knife
so the honed edge of the blade could take a bite

clean through the stalk of burr, severing its life
while missing its nurturing twin, the stem of bean
being pushed aside by the inevitable strife

the strong always win unless an unforeseen
interference from an even stronger force
interrupts the bullying, re-sets the machine

of nature to a different cycle as in this case
of muscled humans bending, cutting, bending
for every single hill of beans till your face

was rife with dusty sweat, no seeming ending
to the new row he told us was half a mile
or so of drudging labor, we were hardly listening

when he said we'll have a rest at the end of this file
of stubborn green tough sons of bitches,
but when he said it again we started to smile

cause he added we'd have ten minutes to get off our haunches
lie flat in solid comfort, sip some cool
aqua from the canvas bottle, feel no crunches

of dry clods underfoot. But we were fools
cause at the end of the row there he lay
having quickly worked his way there a full

eight minutes before, so after a stay
of two minutes at most, "We've had our break
so get off your asses let's start to make our way

through four more rows, it ain't a piece of cake
in case you hadn't guessed by now." And thus
we three teenage guys got up, aches

and tiredness and heat notwithstanding, because
the crew boss man with the power said we must
and where else near that small town could boys

like us who had no money that hot August
get some? I had a quick insight into the bean's
spirit, controlled by the more potent burr,
wishing for a readjustment of the grand machine.

HOEING SOYBEANS II: OLD TURP

One hot afternoon
about half way down
a half-mile swath
of burrs and beans

as the muscled arc
of my trusted corn knife
neared its nadir
it was stopped

by a hard object
not a burr stalk--
my all too clumsily-placed
knee. Ouch, slashed

deep through muscle
boss-man hustled me
(this time he came through)
into the pickup cab

to the wizened coveralled
owner of the farm.
"Come over here son
I've got just the thing,"

We entered a darkened
shed where he rummaged till
I heard delight enter
his voice as he produced

a hoary can half full
of sloshing murk. Taking off
his sweated neckerchief,
he held it down the well

of mystery fluid. "This'll do
the trick," his throaty voice
smiled even more,
the smell seemed

that of very long-standing
turpentine. "Old turp's the best
for deep, serious wounds like this,"
as he dobbed it smartingly

on my uncoy gash.
O Lord let the stinging cease
biting my teeth of course
uncrying midwest male and all,

"It smarts
cause it kills them wily germs
that's what it does,"

he dobbed till the bleeding
almost stopped, then he tied
a dirty rag around
my pain-throbbing knee
and back to hoeing I went,

with the blithe thanks
only a wholesome
small-town Iowa boy
would give in such a plight

unaware how lucky I was
that a modest scar would stand
as the only lasting memorial
to two life lessons not yet learned
that sweaty, turgid afternoon.

FLORIDA JACK

Splash of wake-up water
nothing like it after
thirteen to fifteen hours
unloading peas into boxes
carting boxes of peas
to the weigh station
carefully pouring
boxes of peas
into the hopper
so the conveyer belt
would carry them
in their pea-green finery
up, up then sideways
into the canning machinery.

Cleanup crew:
Scruffy Florida Jack
half-year deserter
of wife and kid,
me clean-cut Iowa boy
rubber-suited -hatted -gloved
Jack and his assistant
spick-ing-and-spanning
the lower deck
I and my assistant
on the upper floor
cooly chasing
every last sonovabitch
remnant pea

down the drain--
both assistants
out and off to bed,

Play time spray time!
Jack having at me
a fairly good burst
of cold nozzled water
I watching for chances
letting him have it
full on his rubberized chest,
enlivening splash into his face
both of us now fully awake
for the only time
in the twenty-four-hour cycle,
getting warmed up
by getting cooled off
for what life at that stage
was all about.

Surely each daily
semi-zombied
fifteen hours
was really
resting-up
for our quickened
nightly (a.m.) battles,

for by the third week
we felt already beyond
apprentice water fencers
as we dodged, feinted,

moved footwork kneework
backwork handwork
headwork into levels
of martial intricacy
we never knew
were in us,

we had become
horseless knights
jousting with thrusts
counterthrusts
postes, ripostes
of roiling liquid laser,

but that was not the point,
the point was
hitting the guy
so hard-direct in the face
best in the eye
that he, blind-rattled
by water's fury
would be beholden
to one's compassion
for several seconds
of blissful Green Giant
pea plant paradise!

Here and there one or the other
approached this quasi-Nirvana state--
once he caught me a bit off-guard
plastered me hard in the gut
and as I looked down

blast! full in the neck
and as I started to flounder
a cold wet finely-focussed
blow to my face,
but I quickly bent down
danced aside nimbly
counterpunching nicely
with a clear stream to his crotch.

One dawn
about five a.m.
I kept my eye
especially focussed on him:
water-sogged
whiskey-logged
drinking since two
(he usually waited till four),
seeming to lose his usual
remarkably-graceful-with-moderate-booze rhythm,

I kept eye out hopes up
for enacting skilled aggressive moves
when he caught my left shoulder
with a sloppy side-swipe,
I ducked and replied to his knees
hoping he'd look down
be slow to raise his noggin--
he still had some trickiness
bringing up his hose full force
before he looked up
catching my mid-section
a pretty good swish

but I could tell
his aim was off
so I fake-aimed my hose
toward his left,
and as he lurched
to his right
nailed him square
in the solar plexis
bending him over,

that did it,
now I had him
on his knees--
merciless, I nozzled up
maximum pinpoint force

another burst in his grinning face
and he was down on his back
like an enlarged stink bug
squirming somehow to roll
out of the incessant stream
of brutal water careening
from my unrelenting hose

back and forth from face to chest
I shot at will
had him at my mercy
the surge within me
pure rushing, liquid power
for those few seconds
until, conquest completed,

I got concerned
his moves were slowing,

I unfocussed the hose,
shut it off entirely,
called, "How you doing, Jack?"
Waited a few seconds
suddenly hot inside my black rubber.
Only his feet moved,
more silence.

Then he was kneeling
grog-eyed looking upward, slow--
"Not too bad. You got me good, Chuck,"
his only apparent damage:
Jack Daniels to vocal cords,
leaving him for now
a sly, crazy soprano.

THE VESSEL

"Will you lead us in prayer, Brother Billy Nowell,"
I ask from behind the simple, peeling
oak pulpit, all eyes on me the music leader,
and on the preacher seated behind and to my left,
eyeing the congregation with all the love, ardor
of a hard-struggled convert turned converter.

Brother Billy obliges to discreet amen
chorus, I lead a congregational hymn
smile, nod, step back to my seat, sit down.
Without pretension H.D. Smith, Minister
steps forward to greet the people and offer
to God almighty an opening prayer

that the village of Lott, Texas, sin-laden,
will repent, be washed in the blood, he sits back down.
I direct the choir in a hymn, more prayers are given,
I sing a solo hymn, announcements are made,
and Brother Smith steps forward, face gleaming.

Father of two, wife "not able to work,"
"She has to do her church member visitations,"
he working full-time as maintenance man
at Baylor University, attending full-time,
holding down demanding preacher position,
two-sermons every Sunday, one at prayer-meeting
on Wednesday evening, not to speak of

Sunday School, evening Training Union,
committees, sick visitations, soothing
emotional wounds, spiritual wanderings, trying
to convert Clay, the town plumber and drunk
who has read too much, can sure outthink

anyone there, prefers his home while wife and kids
get the gospel. H.D. had been converted
while duly incarcerated (he never said what for),
in his late thirties, a drunk, verbal abuser,
now changed for real (I never saw a hint
of what he said had been his sinful road).
He has borrowed my Swiss self-winding watch

(forgot his at home today) with a chuckled warning
he's hard on watches. Because your fist
pounds the pulpit? I ask with a smile,
and he with a crinkle of wonder in his eye replies,
No, they sometimes stop on me as the spirit moves.
(I figure it must have happened, once or twice

fluke-wise, by sheer coincidence, lend it him.)
Now the full moment of Truth has come:
Heavy-set, in his forties, full of late-awakened fervor,
he begins with quiet rhythm that will inevitably
in about twenty minutes build, chant-like,
to its musical/spiritual height of intensity.

As he begins to exhort I casually turn my head
from time to time to glance at the clock on the side wall.
As his sermon builds he reaches the climax
with "Only when Satan stops leaving

his muddy tracks through the streets
of Lott, Texas, will Jesus start to be happy
about us, now let the Holy Spirit descend
on all of us, our friends and neighbors!"
The tiny buzz of the wall clock seems palpable
in the brief prayerful silence. 11:47.

Ten minutes later, the sermon over,
final hymn and prayer completed,
his chant-voice descended from its apogee,
we both step through the aisle, wait by the steps
to greet the sinners, I mention my watch. "Tarnation,"
he abruptly remembers, "I forgot to check the time."
He gingerly pulls it down over his hand,
glances at it, hands it over with a silent question,
I in turn look down, give him a knowing squint.
It reads 11:47.

CLAY TAYLOR

Clay Taylor plumber for Lott, Texas,
Population 900 with 90 widows,
Clay Taylor town drunk
Clay Taylor come to church
prays Reverend H.D. Smith with a catch

in his voice. Got to get Clay to services
wouldn't that be a precious gift for Jesus,
and for his wife and daughter faithful
none more so to the Lord of hosts,
both these women uncomplaining, modest

as morning yes sir. As a student at Baylor
with part-time job as Youth and Music Director
for Lott Baptist I also wondered
the same thing, as Sunday after
Sunday for the whole day I'd stay over

between two hours of service in the morning
and two more hours of church and Training Union
in the evening, enjoying excellent Texas
hospitality including mashed potatoes,
southern fried chicken

succulent beyond what this Yankee
could have imagined. And warm congeniality
with frank opinions, disagreements
in a spirit of mutual cordiality,
and Clay's name would come up over coffee,

generous helping of ice cream, rhubarb pie,
dry coughs, nervous adjustment of necktie,
that would be a mighty work
of the Holy Spirit, we should try
harder to witness to him, but he's a sly

one, not only tough when demon rum
has its grip on his whole spirit and brain,
but even when sober, a smart retort
to words of Jesus we share with him
but God can work as a strange and powerful storm

so pray we must and hope Clay will reform
enter church, rise, confess his sins,
humble his way down the aisle to be saved.
And so it went, until the morning
I was invited by Doris Taylor to spend
the whole of Sunday afternoon with them.

In preparation I girded up my loins
half-hoping Clay Taylor would not be home,
but part of me was curious
to see what sort of animal
what brand of clay formed Clay's disposition,
half of myself was ready for confrontation.

He was there all right, and not the least
bit downtrodden-looking or ashamed
as Doris with some nervousness
introduced us. I could sense
as we tried to chat of crops and weather, an edge,

a touch of resentment to his otherwise poised

manner, well-chiselled appearance, resonant
voice. It was the early 60's, so when we sat
down to ham and sweet potatoes
after he bowed his head at Doris's
nudge, and she gave thanks to God for the food,
I began to intone on the state of the world,

hot-shot student spreading truth to the ignorant,
nuclear threat, our civilization could end,
I expected something like "I never
realized how much danger
we are in, you sure learn a lot
in all them there classes you attend,"

or "I don't reckon it's all as bad as that,
you young folks always tend to exaggerate,"
etcetera. But what he replied
was "Other civilizations have died
in the long, involved history of the world."

I stopped chewing my slice of ham,
halted of words. He elaborated
and momentarily I joined in,
listening more, talking less,
it dawning on me only then,
piercing my novice gospelness,
what and why we both had become
in such a situation, time, and place.

UNCLE GERALD

Face the size of an oversized honeydew melon
that each year grew more
partly deflated balloon-like jowls and shakeable
parts but with eyes always electric,
wired with his latest selling job
candy and nuts, vacuum cleaners, men's suits
this time it's the real deal, the shiny nugget
that's bound to emerge from the mined ore
of previous door-to-door ventures

I can still hear the dynamic current rushing
between eyes and voice and body, gesturing,
mouth explaining exactly why this time
it's totally different, bound to succeed,
though now looking back I hear
the nervous desperation in each hopeful surge,
waves of a small lake swishing a bit too hard
on the shore of his deeper spirit.

O but the grilled steak and custom-made eggs
he and Aunt Mary loved to prepare
for their darling Boxer, child to their childlessness
and Uncle in his chef's apron frying shrimp
special burgers loin of pork hashbrowns
enjoying ingestion as much as preparation
his girth's yearly expansion matching that of
the folds in his face.

When I was five, and he and Aunt Mary
swooped me up footed pajamas and all
out of my crib to zoom to the magic of
Riverview Park, Des Moines, the zoomiest moment
of which was my front seat on the roller-coaster
(o how my folks laughed at my total pallor
"White as a sheet" when it stopped,
my having known for the first time
the pure, uncontaminated thrill of fear)

then and for years afterward I knew somehow
that he must be a whiz of a salesman to always
be promoted to better and better things to sell,
and pay for all that great nourishment and the decent
apartment. Decades later I learned that
Aunt Mary had had a steady position
at the post office all those years,
(She slender, graceful, attractive, with dignity
and, like him, could laugh and chuckle—
though hers was calmer, less driven).

Uncle Jerry, his moniker always from my dad
his older brother, Uncle Jerry or just Jerry—
Jerry and Mary—easiest couple name to remember
on this green earth, we always heard. Jerry
who looked even more like his cramp-minded
mom than did my dad, but who unlike her
was no jealous shrew, hammering nag
who badgered husband Charles Andrew,
kindest spouse and father one could hope for.

First I heard all was not right or even
that there was a physical problem was when
my reticent dad wrote me
Jerry's real bad. I hadn't even known
he was a little bad, nor did my dad
even when asked by letter, elaborate on
what the bad precisely was.
Two letters or so later, Jerry's gone.
Funeral's Thursday. We'll be driving down.

To this day I still don't know what took him,
whether it might have been related to his
surging electricity in eyes and frame,
the always-too-heavy body, the swollen
honeydew head or what.
Next time I have time
I'll have to write my cousin
and find out.

TO MY NEW GRANDDAUGHTER ANYA

As Moon Spirit
circle dances
Mother Earth
turns
wobbles
sometimes roars
around Grandfather Sun,
in cycles that turn
and re-turn
on, on

So in the cycle
the turning
of wondrous creation
like shimmer of song
little Anya
you have come,
wide-eyed and
savoring your thumb.

But whether turning
wobbling
roaring
toward your
own Mother Moon
or Father Sun,
you are precious
as the mantle of the morning,
little one.

NANCY MIRABILE

When they come to you for learning
how voice can express delight, yearning,
the fullest range of thought, emotion
from rumination to devotion,

to ground them so they can perform
their best, you lead them beyond the norm
of excellence they could conceive
to a land one must live in to believe

it could be real. Breath, focus,
open throat, the grounding locus
of right technique for vocal expression
you show with clarity, warmth, passion,

but go far beyond with rare insight
to integrate them with the light
of what it is they sing about
and how and why, until a shout

of jubilant recognition swells
from deep inside them, and dispels
shadows of insecurity,
leaving them knowing they can be free

to sing with truth, fidelity.
I know because the them is me,
and with all this comes heart's caress,
and boundless love, and gentleness.

NANCY'S HANDS

They undulate into the keys,
knowing, deft discoverers
of much this black and white
two-levelled terrain
leaves dumb to others.

Their fingers probe
with necessary force, tenderness
the voiced textures,
hammered resonance
of strings.

Face, shoulders
body wholly
move with hands
a oneness
into the keys
as if you were touching
the apt nerves
of a body just now enlivened,
ready to sing
as your caresses will,

bringing forth
from this slumbrous animal
laughter, cries,
shouts, whispers,
awed near-silences:

cellos, horns,
timpani hoofbeats,
fluted birds:
an orchestra
it did not know it contained

until the measured passion
of your graced and slender instruments
awaken it to the beauty within itself.
Awaken it to the beauty within you.

WATERS

In the country in which I found myself
there appeared to be no clock,
and since an especially perverse elf

gnome or ogre with whom I could not speak
had apparently left me there
without the least ability to make

sense of my surroundings, an atmosphere
of Poe-etic despair and dread
tinged each house in that dark city, a fear

of whatever. I muscled on ahead
anyway, now feeling
that those brownstoney structures and thin, dead

streets with twisted lamp poles would surely bring
me the necessary clues,
the melody however baroque that would sing

me into tonic key. From behind, noise
swept closer. As I dodged
to avoid the small wheeled cart, to my surprise

it was one of my best childhood friends. I called
as loudly as I could (soft)
he screeched to a stop, started toward me, looked

intently, turned, continued his coast
down what was now a steep hill
whose incline forced my feet (now bare) to run fast.

Everything whizzed by, a rigamarole
of blurred twists and rough stone,
my friend must be beyond the next twisted pole

that twist in the street I would not be alone
in this winding plummet.
As I careened around the corner, the scene

was an identical aggregate
of darkish ruin.
But even while speeding I hoped

that very soon I would feel
as in this precipitous poem
the reassuring, cool
taste and fragrance of home.

THE TEENAGE VILLAGE

In this village of younger teenagers
I was one of them
not especially unpopular
until time somehow wore on
and somehow it and a premature
strangely configured beard
wore on my popularity and the esteem
I had--in things that were said

here and there astray behind
and around where I was.
In shadows the scene of ensuing action:
a maze noir-like greenish grey
where a short girl the more strange
she looked the more frightened
she was the more frightened
I feeling a stranger became,

for most of the strangeness was
she too was sprouting dark
stubbly grotesquely growing
whiskers which however refused to climb
north of the hang of her lower lip
so she kept her face half hidden
by living inside a grey garbage can,

only her small eyes peering
into dour darkness.
I could no longer stand

this *Village Noir*. I flowed through
the crowded processions
of hazy faces like mercury liquid
whose presence quickly becomes an absence
because it nowhere adheres, soaks in.

So I ran into new environs
where soon I blazed and shone
un-grey-like into a full man.
My return to the scene
must have been inevitable.
The sight of me beard and all
tall and strideful of mien
sent a fright
through the night,

straggles of grey starings
parting like rags of mist
as I lifted the frightened
wraith-thin girl
out of her self-confinement,
the full squint of her eyes upon mine
no trace of stubble on her chin.

ECHOES, INTUITIONS

Sitting on beds chatting
wife daughter self
austere motel room
venetian blinds-striped dusk
we knew without message
on radio TV phone

large enemy jets
would begin to bomb,
soundless as possible
we slipped to the rug
waiting for its beginning

in a few seconds
flash, explosion,
crashes of falling roofs walls everything
outside us it seemed,
we knew surely
encroaching thunder

would soon be upon us.
Minutes passed how many
only a clattering echo sounded
ever more dimly
into silence
we sensed

the menacing others
had changed position,
were now
in the room
on the other side
of our cardboard-thin wall,
suspecting
we were here,
if they heard us
they would come in.

How long
that strange liquid suspension?
In time the others
must have gone,
suspecting nothing:
long silence in dark totality
leaving us
for a time
our still-quickened mortality.

COIL

When coiled mass whirls it might have been
a bit of DNA inside ant or fly
it might have been the same in dog
or human it may be tightly-wound
dog chasing its tail it may be Whirling
Dervish getting in touch with Mystery
it may be merely lit coil whose smoke

is acrid to mosquitoes and other small pests
it may be burning firework ripping large
circle in night sky beautiful
as it rises apogees dies it may be
spiral nebula of nearly incalculable
immensity sigh-inspiring grandeur beauty
or decorated top spun by awe-struck child

or on art gallery wall
a thing that turns,
dizzying human optics,
or any kind of
whorled
spring
that anyone
or thing
chooses
to spin

but if tightly wound like spring of old watch
or any such kind of compressed thing
it may suddenly spring
as if shockingly enlarging itself
in an instant tearing hurting
whatever whoever is too near Whing!
Ping! Out of itself in a minisecond
it may stop heart of heart-stoppable, send

frisson into spine of even the non-frisson-
-prone vertigoing them not pausing--
leaping Zoom! upward or downward menacing
from its circumference flinging outward sucking
inward. If living DNA so performed--
gene whirlwind or whirlpool, if spiral nebula
so acted--astro-tornado or maelstrom--this poem
and all others being swirled in
whirled out of
minds
would never
be

MINGLINGS

When an apparent lemon rind
in final stages of decomposition
surged with the in-tide onto the hot sand,
a substantial clam in its last minutes of dying
found its shell mouth nudging this new neighbor,

and with inspiration born of desperation
the mollusk forced a wider aperture,
letting its last vital juices mingle
with those of its new citrussy friend,

a novel commingling that caused smoke
and fumes to spiral ever thicker,
more intensely, grittily continuing to exhale
though moved shoreward by the seawind.

How long until it continued is unknown,
but some have said it made the snuggled beings
glow with uncanny luminescence
all the way into their final dim and demise,

and that the scent that arose and pervaded for a time
the entire beach and shoreline,
was the most exhilaratingly pungent
that part of the world has ever known.

E—UI

Bore
dom.
Why not
boreheit
boreness?

Or leave out
the BOR
entirely.
funk dom.
unk dom.
At least here
the sound
is more
onomatopoetic, no?

Bore recalls
the OR
that Poe
declared
most forlorn
thus nevermore Lenore, etc.

Surely boredom
is other than
forlorn.
Much less
if truth be told.
Forlorn has a bit of fire,

forlorn would raise boredom
up a notch at least
perhaps to
interesting.

A step below is
ennui.
An even more
leaden deadened
funk dom.

Why when one
is under a ton
of boredom
can one not just
by willing suddenly
push up to soar-dom?
Why when held down
by ennui
cannot one
by wished effort
flee?

Or at least take a drill
and bore
a big hole
in boredom:
bo om
boom.

Or do the same
to ennui
e ui
ahwe.

ah we
can not.
bo dom
ho hum.

THE MANATEE MISSILE

will be the most advanced
yet in our burgeoning arsenal
though shaped for sheerest
aerodynamic thrusting speed
unlike its more bulbous slower namesake.

It has this appellation for three reasons:
First: the name is derived from Latin manatus
which means provided with hands
and our missile will be so controllable
as to seem literally hand-guided
which honors its namesake also designed
for maximum maneuverability
though ours is in air not murky waters.

Second: its intent
is friendly, peaceful.
Only when it senses a threat
will it strike, but then with warrior courage.

Third: to our sleek creation
the Manatee brings an aura
of noble ancientness
and like its counterpart
is the product of years
(eons in its case)
of clever evolution,

for instance like the whale
from land back to water etc.
and on into changes it made
because of our boat propellers
and other man-made items and habits
plus its now-believed closeness
to the dignified elephant
which only adds to its layered mystery.

Our efficient machine
though its progenitors
go back only decades
to the Redstone Rocket, etc.,
reflects a more sophisticated
acceleration in its stages
adaptations refinements
than was possible with God
or mere chance.

Thus because we grieve
the inevitable demise
of the organic version
to make way for
the necessary all-new
Cape Dolphin launching site,

we name our weapon Manatee
as we anticipate test launches
when its rounded conical head
will penetrate the putative
enemy's strongest defenses
soundlessly nuzzle itself

against them, exploding
with mesmerizing
rush and rage
that will do credit
to its distinguished lineage.

ELEPHANT WORM

Elephant worm
elephant worm
word of the day
the song you play

Elephant worm
elephant worm
they say it unbinds
the ridge of your mind

Elephant worm
so terrific
when you are tense
the best soporific

Yet elephant worm
such versatile use!
when you are juiceless
it gives you the juice.

It's the rising sun
if that turns you on,
Elephant worm
is a lovely Chaconne,

a broadway hit
a top-ten tune
a glamorous garment
a trip to the moon

It's father and mother
all rolled into one,
It's God and Nirvana
the setting sun

Everyone's got one
you really should too
you don't think you need it
but we know you do.

You thought you were content,
you thought you were happy without it,
but we know better, friend,
you're suffering, no doubt about it.

This wonderful elephant worm
will keep you in touch, connected:
who cares if you know who you are--
you'll never feel neglected.

THE CHRISTMAS SPIRIT

If I wander enough
through these scenic aisles,
an Odysseus recherché,
inspiration, as for him,
will surely strike today.

Now take a gander over here—
a new tool chest chock-full
of goodies. I think Dad's other two
have begun to accumulate
so much dust they don't look new,

almost unused in the cellar
for, respectively, five and eight
Christmases. Probably some rust
since Dad's last workbench project
wiggled and wobbled before it went bust,

Dad a handyman with cussing
and all kinds of ultimatums,
hurting his fists on the workbench, etc.
So this new tool chest beauty
might almost be like a change-life mantra,

should be the very thing
so he can be ready when
an unlikely but still possible
(you never know these days)
crisis arises when he, unflappable

despite the extreme direness
of our situation will pull out
that 33/64-inch socket,
insert it, turn it quick as a flash,
rescuing us like Davy Crockett

from cliff-hanger panic. Besides,
these tools are shiny and bright,
in a classy brown wooden chest—
will look right spiffy under the tree,
make Dad's eyes light up with zest,

that my god how'd you guess what I wanted
gleam. Besides, I know he's expecting
shirts socks ties pantaloons
which would raise his eye glow
only a little, considering he owns

ties, thirty-six, assorted
sock pairs forty-seven
shirts enough to encumber
a small dinosaur, and trousers
of vast uncertain number.

Now for Mom—Well, she's
"hard to buy for," has all she needs
of kitchenware, jewelry and such,
and she doesn't seem to be into
handyman tools much,

But wait--pullover sweaters
on special! I'll get her one,
the variation will be nice
from the fifty-four she has,
And you sure can't beat the price!

Besides, this shade of mauve
would be perfect for her complexion!
By god I've done it again--
gifts that show true affection.

THE ARTFUL CASHIER BAGGER

asks politely to see the shopper's card,
even if there is a trundle of customers
trundling up behind the current one,
who hopefully is not staring
too beady-eyed
at items/prices as they appear,

asks would you like plastic or paper
(not paper money ha ha heard
many times from trundling shoppers),
then the scanning remembering
prices of produce etc
(why do the damned stores change them
so goddamned often) but let me punch in
the figures anyway, bag while punching
almost as one quick swipe/snatch/placement,

but ah the arrangement within the enclosures
hard on the bottom fragile on top
everything in one bag ok?
wettish things, coldish things,
potentially-from-air-condensation things
plastic for this?
this this this this
(deep in my mind who gives a piss

specially at end of longish routinish
mood-cloud days
who really gives a rats ass

whether onions are on sale
for three cents less than normal
or paper or plastic schlaper, schlastic
I dont give an ants fart
if one of these
less than polite faces
shoves paper plastic
raincoat poncho newspaper etc
up his so to speak
collective intestinal crap bag).

The authentic Artful Cashier Bagger
will tamp down such thoughts,
such feelings,
ferment no such brute obscenities
or if ferment begins
not let them rise
like jaundiced worms
up through the gorge
into the voicebox
out of the mouth.

No sir the artful one
will scan and organize
cashier/bagging
into a higher aesthetic
punch in the numbers gently
after asking paper plastic card etc
(lasticer caper lard) no wait
the ACB will not
verbally slip but will

concentrate mightily
smile readily
organize splendidly
so the customer will find
upon reaching home
no cause for complaint
and will praise said ACB

to the food emporium honcho
who will reward said ACB
who will rise to honcho,
raise the bar
to more formidable heights
of cashierbaggingness.

Then when his/her charges have
finally vaulted over
will smile as he informs
his most artful ACB's
that new robot bagger/cashiers
have even more fully
fulfilled his functional,
artistic ideals: because they intone:

Have a good day
Thanks for shopping here
always with unwavering
shimmering courtesy,
so goodbye my comrades my lovelies
let me use this occasion
to show I'm a caring doer,
by awarding you AJP appellation:
Artful Job Pursuer.

DE--

Scrambling the scramblers
de-coding the de-coders
de-programming the de-programmers
de-virusing the de-virusers
de-briefing the de-briefers

de-clarifying the de-clarifiers
de-truthing the de-truthers
de-reductionizing the reductionists
de-constructing the deconstructionists
de-dogmatizing the dogmatists

de-bottom-lining the bottom-liners
de-interfacing the interfacers
de-impacting the impacters
de-quantifying the quantifiers

de-beautifying the de-beautyists
de-prettifying the prettifiers
de-grandeuring the de-grandeurists
de-creating the de-creators
de-naturalizing the de-naturalists

de-mystifying the de-mystifiers
de-idealizing the de-idealizers
de-moralizing the de-moralists
damage-controlling the damage-controllers
de-stabilizing the de-stabilizers

de-masting the de-masters
de-feminizing the de-feminists
de-masculizing the de-masculists

de-braining the de-brainers
de-brainstorming the brainstormers
brainwashing the brainwashers

de-stay-in-touching the stay-in-touch-ers
de-videoizing the vidiots
de-gullibilizing the gullibilites
de-responsibilizing the de-responsibilites
de-parisitizing the parasites
de-facating the fakerites

slandering the slanderers
demonizing the demonizers
de-venoming the venomists
de-jingoing the jingoists
de-xenophobizing the xenophobists
de-bilitating the debilitators
de-stroying the destroyers

IL MAGNIFICO

I Pineapple Magnifico
parade down Lushlife Boulevard
holding high my dignity
so my demeanor will not be marred.

I strive to match or exceed
the braggart Banana Baron,
garish Grapefruit Grandee
Lords Lime and Lemon

and their entourage, tart and seedy!
To the proud Prince of Plantain
the mere Mayor of Mango
I show a masque of disdain

while inside feeling dicey.
But great relief is in sight--
The mere Earl of Elderberry
won't dare to put up a fight

for the golden ring we all covet.
But wait--that Alderman of Apple
's station is beneath contempt
and his pedigree--from a raffle

no doubt, with name slip stolen.
And further, there'd better not be
presumptuous Ottomans of Orange
or I shall have to make free

with my rough-edged head armour,
and that would be skewering trouble
right here on Lushlife Boulevard
which might threaten to burst the bubble

cause a melee we all would hate,
for The King of Kiwi awaits I am told
behind the gates of his Palm Palace,
in his courtyard all of green and gold

where the hidden, final truth will be shown--
one of us marchers no doubt me
for strength of stem and ripeness of head
He will designate Lord Justice of Kiwi,

a scrumptious addendum for any peer
of any striped textured plant,
and there is further reward to come,
"to grace the palate of the Grand Tyrant."

Palate sounds a lot like palace,
and to grace it! an honor that nearly
makes my meat and fluids flow
in a juicy generous gesture of merely
humble thanks that such He should bestow
on his faithful Pineapple Magnifico.

MAY 1, 2005

(With a nod to W.H. Auden)

Faces full of good cheer
Get through their average day,
Laptop and cell stay on
Or TV must always play.
All the devices conspire
To give one's space the shine
Of a luminescent dream,
Lest we should see where we are,
Lost in a shadowy cave,
Children afraid of the light
Who have never been happy or brave.

MR. BURNSIDE

As Mr. Burnside
lounges in his lounger,
thinking of his sideburns
of motes of dust
he has just steam-wiped
from his spectacles,

wondering if there is
some thread
of connection
between them

He tentatively touches
the furry burns
fingering ear-hold spines
of glasses--

yes, both there, intact
he is seeing clearly,
his cheeks and jawline
insulated warmly

Touch and sight
integrated parts
of a single cranium
increasingly difficult
to define
though at times like these
easily sensed,

But times like these
come less and less
as books books
come more and more,
what is in them undermined
while being taken in,

as he becomes
a master of substance:
taking it apart
down to its last
molecular thought.

On his spectacles now
new encloudings
of dust motes,
his fingers
seem to be brushing
a sideburn's
furry ghost.

ON THOSE FIELDS

On those fields
on those spring fields
on those well-sprayed spring
fields where corn was cut and thrown
away where now stubble stands in early spring
still mostly frozen partly soaked by melting
snow, pockets of ice inside the stalks
in folds of desiccated leaves in
so many places out of sight
impossible to see from
row's end

On those same fields
where field mice spiders
the occasional raccoon and
possum seeking moldered grain
as a felt delicacy after winter's stern
disclipline of body and spirit, mind and
sinew, on those level plains unseen
by all but beings warm, friendly
to mother earth there lurk

Shadow monoliths
first barely visible in fog
of dawn at its stark crispest
tremoring at the stubble's edge
as a faint vibration that sends rodents
quietly slinking for cover, hungry holes
far preferred much loved over these

strange shadows steadily march-
dancing through the remnants
left over from an especially
voracious winter,

moving inward
with ever broader
phalanxes an army
expanding increasing
as it stodges its way through
though farmers accustomed to
indiscriminately cutting ploughing
the earth mother aver they see nothing
but some unusual morning wind rustling
rustling though a young child says look look
over there and now there and there and coming
here closer almost all over everywhere now dad
and now even dad and two hired hands must
squint their eyes to shut out diminish the
cloudy presences must try to shut their
ears to the wind's voice as it rushes
toward around beneath into them
their faint shudder muffled
moanish whisper inward
they will never again
be the same.

POOL

White globe over table.
Weight-comforting
small numbered

sphere ships over
flat green sea--
some still
others embattled

sky glow flickers
storm-like with shadows
as they loiter meander careen collide

undestroyed confined
within the conflict zone
by safe horizons of ocean

destined
to be swallowed
into respective abysses
one by one.

EVOLUTION I

sedimentation
germination
vegetation
animation

fascination
agitation
copulation
procreation

rumination
habituation
ostentation
consternation

dissipation
discoloration
termination
sedimentation

EVOLUTION II

sedimentation
germination
vegetation
animation

fascination
agitation
copulation
procreation

rumination
examination
meditation
preparation

culmination
termination
transformation
levitation

OUTCROPPING

a bit of a climb
quite far up
almost to the top of the mesa
on that stone outcropping facing west
one feels at dusk soothingly cool wind

ones body touches
warm platform rock
with cool air moving,
mix of being not unlike the struggled
blending of jagged purple dark with rounded light

gold that sends sun
splaying melting into sea
edge of distant mountain outward down
out of sight its diffused light still vying
with violet shade into beyond its slow
dying like the stone heat
hanging on against
ones body long
into zephyrs
cold

IF ARIEL DANCED ON THE MOON

If Ariel danced on the moon
hard surfaces would begin to move
fissures would appear, widen,
deepen in cracking rhythm

matching movement tempo of dance
chasming downward deeper musical
pitches blending in counterpoint
with treble of smaller rocks pinging,

dance building toward first climax
trickles of moisture rippling out
into streamlets. Pools forming
at apex of pas de deux, waves

in furling crescendo splashing sound
on craters' shore where small creatures form
jelly belly up from fresh-made sea acceleration
of life evolution quickly complexifying

till the land leaden toad emerges high on the dry
rocky embankment. As Ariel dances with ever more
passion, wart after wrinkled wart begins to move
vibrate dissever itself they float then fly as specks

of shimmering dancing light in the lunar sky!
Moving toward, around the dancing form,
their former host amazed feels itself the excitement,
opens its now sparkling eyes, pirouettes

most untoadlike over the ground. The Ariel dancer
engraces his arms, turning, leaping
and always no matter how high he soars,
floats back down to the ever more fecund surface.

Even known gravitational laws of luna
do not apply here to him because Ariel--
stunningly magical Arial--is dancing
dancing on what is no longer and never can be
again a dry, cold mass of stone.

Charles Bachman holds a Ph.D. in Comparative Literature from Indiana University, and is a Professor at Buffalo State College, where for almost twenty years he has specialized in Native American Literature. He has also had an active career in western New York as an operatic baritone, performing twenty-five major roles in operas, operettas, and musicals, as well as giving many recitals and being guest soloist with orchestras including the Syracuse Symphony and the Buffalo Philharmonic. Periodicals where his poetry has appeared include *The Carolina Quarterly* and *The Kansas Quarterly.* He is married to pianist/vocal coach Nancy Townsend.

ISBN 1412090121

9 781412 090124